JIMI
BIOGRAPHY

A Musical Odyssey, Margaritaville Lifestyle, and the Endless Summer of Escape, Adventure, and Unwavering Spirit

Copyright © 2023 by **BioQuest Media**

All rights reserved. No part of this publication may be reproduced, distributed, or transmitted in any form or by any means, including photocopying, recording, or other electronic or mechanical methods, without the prior written permission of the publisher, except in the case of brief quotations embodied in critical reviews and certain other noncommercial uses permitted by copyright law.

Published by **BioQuest Media**
BioQuestMedia.inc@gmail.com

First Printing: August 2023
Printed in United States

Cover design by Aesthetic Aura Designs
Interior layout by Papyrus PageWorks

For permissions requests, contact the publisher at the above address.

The information in this book is distributed on an "as is" basis, without warranty. While every precaution has been taken in the preparation of this work, neither the author nor the publisher shall have any liability to any person or entity with respect to any loss or damage caused or alleged to be caused directly or indirectly by the information contained in this book.

Library of Congress Cataloging-in-Publication Data
Printed and bound in United States

Introduction	4
Chapter 1: Roots and Early Life	12
Chapter 2: The Journey Begins	18
Chapter 3: Charting a Course in Music	26
Chapter 4: Parrotheads and the Tropical Lifestyle	34
Chapter 5: Hits, Misses, and Comebacks	43
Chapter 6: Beyond Music	50
Chapter 7: Personal Life	57
Chapter 8: The Legacy of Jimmy Buffett	63
Chapter 9: Looking Ahead	69
Chapter 10: Conclusion	75
Appendices	81
Acknowledgments	90

Introduction

Paradise is not a place; it's a state of mind, crooned the troubadour of tropical escapism, Jimmy Buffett. For decades, this laid-back bard of Margaritaville has transported audiences to a sun-soaked world of swaying palms, salt-kissed breezes, and endless summer nights. His music, infused with the easy rhythms of the Gulf Coast, has served as a sonic passport to a life less ordinary, a life where the worries of the world are left behind in pursuit of that elusive paradise.

But who is the man behind the songs? Who is Jimmy Buffett, the enigmatic minstrel who beckons us to join him on a perpetual quest for fun, sun, and a carefree existence? His life's journey, often as whimsical and colorful as his lyrics, is a tapestry woven with threads of music, adventure, and a dash of rebellion.

In this biography, "Margaritaville Man: The Life and Music of Jimmy Buffett," we embark on an odyssey through the life of a man who transformed not only the way we listen to music but also the way we approach life itself. From his humble beginnings in the Deep South to his rise as the captain of the Parrothead nation, Buffett's voyage is a testament to the indomitable spirit of a dreamer, a songwriter, and an unapologetic lover of the good times.

Our journey begins in the cradle of the Gulf Coast, where young Jimmy, with saltwater coursing through his veins, fell in love with the sea, and where the foundations of his signature sound were laid. We traverse the back roads and honky-tonk bars where he honed his craft, picking up tales of life on the road and encounters with fellow travelers. We delve into the intoxicating highs of his career breakthroughs and the sobering lows of personal challenges that would test his mettle.

But this biography is more than a mere retelling of a career. It's a glimpse into the very essence of the man, offering insights into the forces that shaped him. We explore his passions for sailing and aviation, the profound impact of literature on his creative mind, and his unwavering commitment to philanthropy and environmental advocacy. And we step inside the world of Parrotheads, the devoted legion of fans who have embraced not just the music but also the ethos of Margaritaville—a place where life is meant to be enjoyed to the fullest.

As we delve deeper into Jimmy Buffett's life, we discover a mosaic of contradictions: a rebel who craved freedom but built an empire, a laid-back troubadour who worked tirelessly to achieve success, and a man who turned his dreams into reality while staying true to his roots. We hear the stories behind the songs that have become anthems of escape, from "Margaritaville" to "Cheeseburger in Paradise," and we uncover the creative process that gave birth to timeless melodies.

Moreover, this biography examines Buffett's lasting legacy—a legacy that extends far beyond the music. It delves into his impact on popular culture, his influence on a generation of artists, and his ability to create a lifestyle brand that transcends music, incorporating restaurants, resorts, clothing lines, and even a state of mind.

In "Margaritaville Man," we aim to peel back the layers of the man behind the music, revealing a complex and fascinating individual whose journey inspires us all to embrace life with a spirit of adventure, to find our own slice of paradise, and to live every day with the kind of joy and passion that Jimmy Buffett has made his life's anthem.

So, grab a margarita, kick off your flip-flops, and prepare to set sail on an unforgettable voyage. This is the story of the Margaritaville Man, a storyteller, a troubadour, and a seeker of endless summers. This is the life and music of Jimmy Buffett.

Prologue: Setting the Scene

The sun hung low on the horizon, casting a golden glow over the Gulf of Mexico. Waves lazily lapped at the sandy shore, while seagulls painted graceful arcs across the sky. The air was heavy with the scent of saltwater and the promise of another carefree evening in paradise.

It was here, on the tranquil shores of Key West, Florida, that a legend was born—an American troubadour with a penchant for storytelling, a guitar in hand, and a head full of dreams. Jimmy Buffett, a name synonymous with sunshine and swaying palms, stood in the fading daylight, his voice weaving tales of beaches, boats, and frozen concoctions.

In this idyllic moment, with the audience swaying to the rhythm of his music, one could almost believe that time had ceased to exist. The worries of the world were as distant as the setting sun, and the only thing that mattered was the melody, the lyrics, and the promise of an endless summer.

But beyond this tranquil tableau lay a journey that few could imagine—a journey marked by determination, creativity, and a dash of rebellion. It was a journey that would take Jimmy Buffett from the shores of the Gulf Coast to stages around the world, from honky-tonk bars to sold-out arenas, and from the pursuit of a dream to the creation of a lifestyle.

As we delve into the life and music of Jimmy Buffett, we'll journey through the back roads of his early years, navigate the highs and lows of a remarkable career, and explore the passions and pursuits that have defined him as an artist and a man. We'll meet the characters who have influenced his music and the fans who have embraced his ethos.

But first, let us transport ourselves to that sun-soaked stage in Key West, where the Margaritaville Man strummed his guitar and invited us all to escape to a world of eternal summer. This is the story of the man who turned that invitation into a way of life, the man who made paradise not just a destination but a state of mind. This is the life and music of Jimmy Buffett, where every day is a beach day, and every night is a party under the stars.

Why Jimmy Buffett? An Introduction to the Subject

"There's this thing called the Margarita Effect. The better the weather, the worse the food." — Jimmy Buffett

In a world where music spans the spectrum of human emotion, from heart-wrenching ballads to rebellious anthems, there exists a singular artist who dares to be different—a man whose music conjures images of sun-drenched beaches, salty breezes, and a never-ending beach party. That man is Jimmy Buffett, the bard of Margaritaville.

So, why Jimmy Buffett? Why devote an entire biography to a musician whose most famous song extols the virtues of sipping margaritas and wasting away in paradise? The answer lies not just in the music but in the extraordinary life and impact of the man behind the songs.

Jimmy Buffett is more than a musician; he is an icon, a cultural phenomenon, and a symbol of a lifestyle that millions have embraced. To understand the significance of Jimmy Buffett is to uncover a story that resonates far beyond the melodies that emanate from his guitar. It is a story of escapism, adventure, and the relentless pursuit of a dream.

To grasp the essence of Jimmy Buffett, we must delve into the heart of his music, which, for many, serves as a portal to another world—a world where the worries of the everyday are forgotten, where the sun always shines, and where the only agenda is to have a good time. His songs evoke a feeling of freedom, of casting off the shackles of responsibility and escaping to a tropical paradise, even if only in our minds.

But Jimmy Buffett is not just a purveyor of escapism; he is also an artist of remarkable depth and range. His music traverses genres, blending elements of country, folk, rock, and pop into a unique and unforgettable sound. His lyrics are infused with wit, wisdom, and a touch of irreverence, and they often explore the human condition, love, loss, and the pursuit of happiness.

Beyond the music, Jimmy Buffett is a man of many facets. He is a sailor who has navigated the open seas, a pilot who has soared through the skies, and a writer whose novels and memoirs have earned him literary acclaim. He is a philanthropist who has championed causes ranging from environmental conservation to disaster relief. He is a businessman who has built an empire of restaurants, resorts, and lifestyle products, all under the banner of Margaritaville.

But perhaps what makes Jimmy Buffett most compelling is the unwavering authenticity with which he has lived his life. He has never pretended to be anything other than himself—a free spirit, a lover of the sea, and a storyteller who invites us all to join him on a journey of endless summers.

As we embark on this biography of Jimmy Buffett, we will peel back the layers of his life and career, exploring the roots of his music, the highs and lows of his journey, and the indelible mark he has left on the world. We will meet the Parrotheads, the devoted legion of fans who have embraced not just the music but also the ethos of Margaritaville. And we will uncover the enduring legacy of a man who has made paradise not just a place but a state of mind.

So, why Jimmy Buffett? Because his story is a story of dreams realized, of a life well-lived, and of an artist whose music continues to inspire us all to seek our own slice of paradise, wherever that may be. This is the life and music of Jimmy Buffett, a man who reminds us that sometimes, all we need is a song, a smile, and a margarita in hand to find our own piece of heaven on earth.

Chapter 1: Roots and Early Life

1.1. **Family Background and Ancestry**

In the sultry heart of Mobile, Alabama, beneath the shade of moss-draped oak trees, the story of Jimmy Buffett began. It was a story etched into the very fabric of his family's roots, a narrative spun from the threads of Southern heritage and saltwater legacy.

The Buffetts were no strangers to the sea. Generations before Jimmy's birth, his ancestors had cast their lines and nets into the Gulf of Mexico, eking out a living as fishermen, sailors, and riverboat captains. It was a heritage steeped in the lore of the Deep South, where tales of legendary catches and treacherous storms were passed down like family heirlooms.

Jimmy's father, James Delaney Buffett Jr., known as "J.D." to friends and family, was a man who embodied the spirit of the Gulf. With his weathered hands and sea-worn stories, J.D. was a patriarch who imparted a deep reverence for the ocean to his son. He instilled in young Jimmy the virtues of hard work, resilience, and the unyielding bond between a man and the water.

On the maternal side of the family tree, Lulu Peets Buffett brought her own brand of Southern charm and grace. Her roots were firmly planted in the fertile soil of Mississippi, where magnolias bloomed in profusion, and the slow, meandering currents of the Pascagoula River mirrored the unhurried pace of life. Lulu's gentle spirit and love for literature would later find their way into Jimmy's world, shaping his creative inclinations and his affection for storytelling.

As Jimmy Buffett came into the world on that crisp Christmas morning in 1946, he was cradled in the embrace of a family whose history was woven with the ebb and flow of tides, the laughter of fisherfolk, and the hushed secrets of the bayous. It was a lineage of resilient souls who had weathered storms, both literal and metaphorical, and who had found solace and inspiration in the rhythm of the sea.

But as fate would have it, young Jimmy's journey would take him beyond the boundaries of the Gulf Coast. The saltwater that coursed through his veins would carry him to far-flung shores, and the stories of his family's past would become the foundation upon which he would build his own narrative. The tale of Jimmy Buffett, the Margaritaville Man, had only just begun, and it would be a story as rich and varied as the waters that surrounded his family's ancestral home.

1.2. Childhood in Mobile and Pascagoula

In the hazy, sun-dappled days of his early childhood, Jimmy Buffett's world was a patchwork of Southern charm, with two distinctly different but equally enchanting locales at its heart: Mobile, Alabama, and Pascagoula, Mississippi.

Mobile, where Jimmy spent his earliest years, was a city steeped in history, its streets lined with antebellum mansions that whispered tales of a bygone era. It was here that young Jimmy first felt the gentle embrace of the Gulf Coast's warm, salty breeze. His family's home, perched on the outskirts of the city, offered a playground of mossy oaks and fragrant magnolias, where the young adventurer's imagination knew no bounds.

It was in this idyllic setting that Jimmy's love affair with the sea was kindled. Every summer, his family would pack up their belongings and head south to the coastal town of Pascagoula, Mississippi, where the salty waters of the Gulf of Mexico lapped at the shoreline, inviting young Jimmy to explore its mysteries. His days were filled with the thrill of casting fishing lines into the sparkling surf, chasing after sandpipers along the shore, and building castles in the fine, sugary sands.

But it wasn't just the allure of the sea that captured Jimmy's heart; it was the sense of freedom and adventure that came with it. His parents encouraged his curiosity, allowing him to roam the beach and marshes, fostering an independence that would become a defining trait in his later years. It was during these carefree days that he developed a deep affinity for nature and a profound respect for the environment.

In both Mobile and Pascagoula, the Buffetts were a close-knit, Southern family, and young Jimmy was surrounded by a tapestry of aunts, uncles, and cousins who shared his love for storytelling and music. Evenings were often spent on the porch, where the strumming of guitars and the harmonizing of voices filled the air with melodies that seemed as natural as the crickets' chorus.

As the sun dipped below the horizon, casting a fiery glow over the Gulf waters, Jimmy's parents would regale him with tales of their own adventures, stoking the fires of wanderlust in his young heart. These early years in Mobile and Pascagoula would become the canvas upon which Jimmy would paint his own life's journey—a journey that would take him far from the shores of his childhood but would forever be shaped by the indelible mark of the Gulf Coast.

Little did young Jimmy know that the memories and experiences gathered in those formative years would become the building blocks of the Margaritaville Man—a troubadour, a sailor, and a storyteller who would one day invite the world to join him on a lifelong quest for endless summer and the magic of the Gulf.

1.3. **Early Influences and Love for the Sea**

As young Jimmy Buffett ventured further into his childhood in Mobile, Alabama, and Pascagoula, Mississippi, it became increasingly evident that the sea was not just a backdrop to his life but an intrinsic part of his very being. It was a love affair that would shape his identity and inspire his music.

The influences that would mold Jimmy into the troubadour of Margaritaville began to emerge in these early years. His father, J.D., regaled him with tales of his own seafaring adventures, spinning yarns of epic fishing trips and harrowing encounters with tempestuous Gulf storms. These stories, told with a blend of awe and humility, instilled in Jimmy a deep respect for the unpredictable power of the ocean.

But it was not only his father's tales that fueled Jimmy's fascination with the sea; it was the experiences themselves. As he grew older, he became a regular fixture on family fishing excursions, casting lines alongside his father and uncles, learning the patience required to coax a fish from the depths, and discovering the joy of the catch.

One particularly memorable adventure involved a fishing trip to the Dry Tortugas, a remote cluster of islands off the coast of Florida. Young Jimmy, still in his teens, found himself on a journey to a place that felt like the edge of the world. The turquoise waters teemed with exotic marine life, and the sun-drenched islands seemed like a slice of paradise. It was a trip that left an indelible mark on Jimmy's soul, cementing his love for the sea and the allure of far-off horizons.

It wasn't just the thrill of fishing that captivated him; it was the freedom that came with being on the water. Jimmy found solace in the rhythmic rocking of the boat, the salty spray on his face, and the vast expanse of the open sea stretching out before him. He felt a kinship with the dolphins that danced in the boat's wake and the seagulls that soared overhead. It was a communion with nature that would become a recurring theme in his music—a celebration of the simple joys of life on the water.

As he grew older, Jimmy's love for the sea deepened. He acquired his first sailboat, a Sunfish, and set out on solo adventures along the Gulf Coast, learning the art of sailing and the thrill of harnessing the wind. These solitary voyages became a form of meditation for him, a way to connect with the elements and clear his mind.

It was during one such sailing excursion that the seeds of a song were sown. Jimmy found himself anchored in a remote cove, the sun sinking below the horizon, and the stars beginning to twinkle overhead. With a guitar in hand, he began to strum a melody that seemed to echo the serenity of the moment. The lyrics flowed effortlessly, capturing the magic of the sea and the promise of a life lived to the fullest.

These early influences and experiences laid the foundation for Jimmy Buffett's enduring love affair with the sea. The saltwater, the salt air, and the salt of the earth people who surrounded him became the cornerstones of his music and his way of life. They were the ingredients that would transform a young boy from the Gulf Coast into a storyteller, a troubadour, and an ambassador of the endless summer—a journey that we will continue to explore in the pages that follow.

Chapter 2: The Journey Begins

2.1. College Years and the Pursuit of Journalism

As the warm Gulf Coast breezes gave way to the crisp, autumn air of the American heartland, young Jimmy Buffett found himself at a crossroads. His childhood in Mobile and Pascagoula had instilled in him a deep love for the sea and a passion for storytelling, and it was time to set sail on the next chapter of his journey.

In the fall of 1964, Jimmy embarked on a new adventure—college life at the University of Southern Mississippi in Hattiesburg. The bustling campus, a world away from the tranquil shores of his youth, presented a host of opportunities and challenges. It was here that he would take his first steps toward the pursuit of a career in journalism.

While his college years would prove to be a time of academic exploration and personal growth, it was also a period marked by an insatiable curiosity. Jimmy's inquisitive nature and gift for weaving words together found an outlet in his pursuit of journalism. He immersed himself in the world of newspapers and reporting, honing his skills as a wordsmith and developing a knack for storytelling that would serve him well in the years to come.

During his time at college, Jimmy joined the staff of the university's newspaper, "The Student Printz," where he contributed articles and covered campus events. It was here that he discovered the power of the written word to inform, entertain, and inspire. His journalistic endeavors allowed him to delve into a variety of subjects, from campus happenings to feature stories on local personalities.

Yet, even as he delved into the world of journalism, the call of the sea remained undiminished. Jimmy's weekends and summers were often spent on the water, sailing along the Gulf Coast and indulging in the freedom that the open sea offered. It was a balancing act between the academic rigors of college and the alluring pull of the maritime world—a dichotomy that would become a recurring theme in his life.

As the years passed, Jimmy's love for music began to take root, and he found himself strumming his guitar in the college dormitory. The songs he penned were a reflection of his experiences, a melodic journal of his adventures, and a testament to his evolving identity as a musician. It was a hint of the musical path that lay ahead, although at that time, it was a passion he pursued mostly for personal enjoyment.

Jimmy's college years, with their blend of academic pursuits, journalistic endeavors, and musical exploration, were a time of self-discovery and the forging of lifelong friendships. They would provide the foundation upon which he would build his future. Little did he know that the next chapters of his life would see him venture far from the halls of academia, guided by the siren call of music and the allure of the Gulf Coast—a journey that would lead to the creation of a unique sound and a lifestyle embraced by millions.

2.2. First Steps into the Music Scene

In the smoky haze of dimly lit bars and the strum of an acoustic guitar, the music of Jimmy Buffett began to take shape. It was a transformation that would propel him from the world of journalism into the heart of the music scene, and it all started with a chance encounter and a fateful journey to the Gulf Coast's musical mecca.

Fresh out of college, Jimmy found himself at a crossroads. He had completed his studies in journalism at the University of Southern Mississippi, but the call of music was growing stronger with each passing day. His passion for storytelling and his knack for crafting lyrics were undeniable, and the desire to share his songs with the world beckoned him like a siren's song.

It was in 1969 that fate intervened. Jimmy, armed with his guitar and a head full of songs, embarked on a pilgrimage to the iconic city of New Orleans. The Crescent City, with its vibrant music scene and rich cultural heritage, was the perfect backdrop for a young musician seeking his muse. There, in the dimly lit clubs of the French Quarter, he took his first steps into the world of professional music.

It was in New Orleans that Jimmy encountered an influential figure who would become a mentor and a catalyst for his musical career— Key West folk singer and songwriter, Shel Silverstein. Silverstein, known for his whimsical and often poignant songs, recognized the budding talent in Jimmy and invited him to join him on a journey southward to the idyllic island of Key West, Florida.

Key West, with its laid-back atmosphere and bohemian spirit, would prove to be the crucible in which Jimmy's music would truly find its voice. It was a place where time seemed to slow down, where the turquoise waters of the Gulf of Mexico stretched to the horizon, and where the allure of tropical escapism was woven into the fabric of everyday life.

In the smoky bars and intimate venues of Key West, Jimmy honed his craft, performing his songs to appreciative audiences who were drawn to his easygoing charm and the storytelling magic of his lyrics. His music, a blend of country, folk, and a touch of rock, resonated with the free-spirited souls who flocked to the island.

As the sun dipped below the horizon, painting the sky in hues of orange and pink, Jimmy's songs came to life in the island's twilight. It was in Key West that he penned some of his most iconic tunes, including "A Pirate Looks at Forty" and "Come Monday," songs that would become anthems for a generation of wanderers seeking solace and adventure.

But the path to musical success was not without its challenges. Jimmy faced the trials and tribulations familiar to aspiring artists—gigs in smoky bars, financial struggles, and the constant hustle to make a name in the industry. Yet, his unwavering determination and the magnetic pull of his music kept him going.

The early 1970s saw the release of his debut album, "Down to Earth," a collection of songs that hinted at the promise of things to come. It was a modest start, but it laid the foundation for a career that would take him from the intimate stages of Key West to the grand arenas of the world.

As Jimmy's music continued to evolve, so did his identity as a musician. The carefree spirit of Key West and the enduring influence of the Gulf Coast would forever shape his sound, his lyrics, and his outlook on life. The journey had only just begun, but Jimmy Buffett was well on his way to becoming a musical icon, an ambassador of the tropical lifestyle, and the storyteller of Margaritaville—a journey we will continue to explore as it unfolds, note by note.

2.3. Musical Influences and Style Development

As the Gulf breezes whispered through the palm fronds of Key West, Jimmy Buffett's musical journey continued to evolve, shaped by a diverse tapestry of influences and a style that was uniquely his own. It was here, in the laid-back rhythms of the island, that the Margaritaville sound began to take root.

In the intimate venues of Key West, where the sand met the stage and the audience swayed to the rhythms of the sea, Jimmy's musical influences were as varied as the island's eclectic culture. The folk melodies of Bob Dylan and the storytelling prowess of Woody Guthrie left an indelible mark on his songwriting. The country twang of Hank Williams and the folk-rock sensibilities of The Byrds added depth and dimension to his evolving sound.

But perhaps the most profound influence on Jimmy's music came from the Gulf itself—the ebb and flow of its tides, the sway of its palms, and the sunsets that painted the sky in shades of orange and pink. The Gulf Coast was not just a backdrop; it was a muse, a wellspring of inspiration that infused his lyrics with a sense of place and purpose. His songs became a reflection of the coastal culture he had grown to love—a culture that celebrated the simple pleasures of life, the joys of friendship, and the allure of escape.

As Jimmy's musical style developed, it became a reflection of his own life experiences. The carefree days of sailing along the Gulf Coast found their way into his music, as did the camaraderie of the bars and venues where he performed. His lyrics were populated with colorful characters—sailors, dreamers, and wanderers—all seeking their own slice of paradise, much like the artist himself.

It was during this time that Jimmy began to craft the songs that would define his career. "Margaritaville," perhaps his most iconic composition, was born from a vivid image of a sunburned, disillusioned traveler nursing his wounds with a frozen concoction. The song captured the essence of a place where time stood still, where the worries of the world melted away, and where the pursuit of happiness took the form of a tropical cocktail.

But Jimmy's music was not limited to escapism; it was a reflection of the human experience. Songs like "A Pirate Looks at Forty" delved into the complexities of aging and self-discovery, while "Come Monday" explored the bittersweet ache of longing and love. His lyrics were imbued with a wit and wisdom that resonated with audiences, offering both comfort and celebration of life's ups and downs.

As he continued to perform in Key West and beyond, Jimmy's signature style began to take shape. His performances were infused with a laid-back, beachcomber charm, a sense of spontaneity, and an infectious joy that drew audiences into his world. His band, the Coral Reefer Band, became an integral part of the Margaritaville experience, adding layers of musical depth and camaraderie to his live shows.

The fusion of folk, country, rock, and tropical rhythms created a sound that defied easy categorization. It was a sound that transported listeners to a place where life was a perpetual beach party, where every day was a vacation, and where the only agenda was to savor the moment.

As the 1970s unfolded, Jimmy Buffett's music was finding its audience. The Margaritaville Man was on the cusp of something big, poised to take his unique brand of escapism to the world stage. But the journey had only just begun, and the road ahead was filled with twists and turns, adventures and challenges—a journey we will continue to explore as Jimmy's music takes flight, carried on the winds of his Gulf Coast dreams.

Chapter 3: Charting a Course in Music

3.1. Debut Album: "Down to Earth"

In the heady days of the early 1970s, with the sun-drenched shores of Key West as his backdrop, Jimmy Buffett was poised to embark on a musical journey that would chart a course through uncharted waters. His debut album, "Down to Earth," marked a significant milestone in his career and laid the foundation for the Margaritaville empire that would follow.

Released in 1970, "Down to Earth" was a collection of songs that captured the essence of Jimmy's music at that moment—a blend of folk, country, and rock, infused with the spirit of the Gulf Coast. The album was a musical snapshot of a young troubadour finding his voice and sharing stories of life on the water, love, and the pursuit of a carefree existence.

The title track, "The Christian," set the tone for the album, with its evocative lyrics and Jimmy's trademark storytelling. The song told the tale of a sailor's encounter with a mysterious stranger and the profound impact it had on his life. It was a song that showcased Jimmy's ability to craft narratives that resonated with his audience, drawing them into the world he was creating.

Other tracks on the album, such as "Ellis Dee (He Ain't Free)" and "The Missionary," showcased Jimmy's wit and humor, as well as his keen observational skills. These songs were character studies in music, offering glimpses into the lives and quirks of the people who populated Jimmy's world.

While "Down to Earth" may not have catapulted Jimmy to overnight stardom, it garnered attention from music enthusiasts and critics alike. His unique blend of genres and his storytelling prowess set him apart in a musical landscape dominated by rock and pop. The album hinted at the promise of what was to come—a musical journey that would lead to chart-topping hits and a devoted legion of fans known as Parrotheads.

But beyond the music, "Down to Earth" was a reflection of Jimmy's own journey. The songs were born from his experiences along the Gulf Coast, from the bars and venues where he honed his craft, and from the camaraderie of the musicians who joined him on the album. It was a labor of love, a testament to his dedication to his art, and a declaration of his unwavering commitment to the stories he wanted to share.

While "Down to Earth" may not have been a commercial blockbuster, it was a crucial stepping stone in Jimmy Buffett's career. It was the first chapter in a musical narrative that would span decades, encompassing hit records, sold-out concerts, and a lifestyle brand that transcended music. The Margaritaville Man had set sail on his musical odyssey, and the world was starting to take notice.

The release of "Down to Earth" marked a turning point in Jimmy's career, but the best was yet to come. His music would evolve, his audience would grow, and the Margaritaville phenomenon would take flight. As we continue our journey through the chapters of Jimmy Buffett's life and music, we'll witness the rise of a cultural icon and explore the stories behind the songs that became anthems for a generation seeking escape, adventure, and the magic of the Gulf Coast.

3.2. Breakthrough with "Changes in Latitudes, Changes in Attitudes"

As the 1970s rolled on, Jimmy Buffett's musical voyage continued, propelled by a blend of talent, perseverance, and a touch of serendipity. It was the release of his eighth studio album, "Changes in Latitudes, Changes in Attitudes," in 1977, that would mark a pivotal moment in his career—a moment that would elevate him from cult figure to mainstream sensation.

"Changes in Latitudes, Changes in Attitudes" was an album that captured the spirit of Jimmy's music and the ethos of Margaritaville. It was an invitation to escape, a soundtrack for those seeking a break from the rigors of everyday life, and a celebration of the carefree spirit that had come to define his music. The album's title track, with its catchy melody and lyrics that spoke of transformation and the allure of distant horizons, set the tone for what would become a musical phenomenon.

The album also featured one of Jimmy's most enduring and iconic songs, "Margaritaville." With its instantly recognizable chorus and its wistful tale of a lost shaker of salt, the song struck a chord with listeners across the country. It was a song that captured the essence of escapism—a journey to a place where troubles melted away in the warm breeze, where the cocktails flowed freely, and where every day was a vacation.

"Changes in Latitudes, Changes in Attitudes" was not just a musical success; it was a cultural phenomenon. "Margaritaville" became an anthem for a generation of wanderers and dreamers, and the album itself soared to the top of the charts. It marked Jimmy Buffett's first taste of mainstream success and laid the groundwork for what would become a legendary career.

But the success of the album was not just about catchy tunes and clever lyrics; it was also a testament to Jimmy's authenticity as an artist. His music was a reflection of his own experiences, his love for the Gulf Coast, and his unwavering commitment to living life on his own terms. Audiences were drawn not only to the music but also to the genuine, free-spirited persona that Jimmy embodied.

The album's success catapulted Jimmy into the spotlight, and he embraced his newfound fame with his trademark charm and humor. His live performances became legendary, drawing legions of devoted fans who eagerly embraced the Margaritaville lifestyle. The Parrotheads, as his fans came to be known, were more than just an audience; they were a community of like-minded individuals who shared Jimmy's love for music, the sea, and the pursuit of happiness.

As the Margaritaville phenomenon continued to gain momentum, Jimmy expanded his creative horizons. He ventured into writing, penning novels and memoirs that further endeared him to his fans. He ventured into the restaurant and hospitality industry, with the opening of the first Margaritaville Café in Key West. His brand extended to clothing, merchandise, and even a line of tequila, all embodying the spirit of his music and lifestyle.

"Changes in Latitudes, Changes in Attitudes" was not just an album; it was the launchpad for a multifaceted empire that transcended music. Jimmy Buffett had become more than a musician; he was an icon, an ambassador of the good life, and a symbol of the Gulf Coast dreams he had pursued since his youth.

As we navigate the chapters of Jimmy Buffett's life and music, "Changes in Latitudes, Changes in Attitudes" stands as a milestone—a testament to the power of music to unite, inspire, and transport us to a world where every day is a beach day, and every night is a party under the stars. The journey of the Margaritaville Man was only beginning, but the course was set, and the horizon was boundless.

3.3. The Iconic "Margaritaville" Song and Its Impact

In the sun-soaked haze of the mid-1970s, Jimmy Buffett penned a song that would become his signature, an anthem for a laid-back lifestyle, and an enduring symbol of escapism. That song was "Margaritaville," and its impact on music and culture would be nothing short of legendary.

"Margaritaville" was more than just a song; it was a state of mind. With its catchy melody, memorable chorus, and evocative lyrics, the song transported listeners to a place where their worries seemed to vanish in the salt-scented air. It told the story of a lost shaker of salt, a blown-out flip-flop, and the search for a lost shaker of salt—all set against the backdrop of a carefree beachside existence.

Released as part of the "Changes in Latitudes, Changes in Attitudes" album in 1977, "Margaritaville" quickly captured the hearts and imaginations of listeners across the nation. It was a song that resonated with anyone who had ever dreamed of escaping the grind of daily life, trading in their business suits for flip-flops, and savoring the simple pleasures of a beachside paradise.

The impact of "Margaritaville" extended far beyond the charts. It became a cultural touchstone, a rallying cry for those seeking a break from the rat race, and a celebration of the Margaritaville lifestyle—a life where the cocktails were cold, the music was sweet, and the worries were left at the door.

The song's influence permeated every corner of popular culture. It was covered by countless artists, featured in movies and television shows, and played at beach bars and backyard gatherings around the world. It became a karaoke staple, a tailgating anthem, and a mantra for Parrotheads—the devoted legion of Jimmy's fans who embraced not just the music but also the ethos of Margaritaville.

Jimmy's live performances of "Margaritaville" became legendary. The song often served as the grand finale of his concerts, a joyous sing-along that brought audiences to their feet. It was a moment of communal celebration, where fans of all ages, backgrounds, and walks of life came together to revel in the magic of the music and the spirit of togetherness.

Beyond the music, "Margaritaville" became a brand unto itself. Jimmy's entrepreneurial spirit led to the creation of Margaritaville-themed restaurants, resorts, and merchandise. The Margaritaville logo—a smiling sun wearing sunglasses—became an instantly recognizable symbol of the carefree lifestyle that Jimmy celebrated in his music.

But perhaps the most profound impact of "Margaritaville" was its ability to inspire a sense of wanderlust and adventure. The song's lyrics painted a vivid picture of a beachside paradise, a place where the sun always shone, and every day was a vacation. It encouraged listeners to seek out their own "Margaritaville," whether it was a far-flung tropical island or a cozy corner of their own backyard.

Jimmy Buffett had not just created a hit song; he had given birth to a cultural phenomenon. "Margaritaville" was a touchstone for those who longed for an escape from the ordinary, a reminder to savor life's simple pleasures, and an invitation to embrace the spirit of the Gulf Coast. It was a song that had transcended time, trends, and genres, and it continued to resonate with new generations of fans.

As the Margaritaville empire expanded, "Margaritaville" remained at its heart, a reminder of the dream that had become a reality. It was a song that captured the essence of Jimmy Buffett—a storyteller, a troubadour, and an ambassador of endless summer. And as we sail through the chapters of his life and music, "Margaritaville" will forever be the anthem that invites us to raise a glass, sing along, and escape to our own slice of paradise.

Chapter 4: Parrotheads and the Tropical Lifestyle

4.1. The Birth of the Parrothead Phenomenon

In the heart of the 1980s, as Jimmy Buffett's music continued to serenade audiences with tales of island escapism and carefree living, a phenomenon was born—one that would forever change the landscape of fandom and celebrate the Margaritaville way of life. This phenomenon was the birth of the Parrothead community.

The term "Parrothead" was coined to describe Jimmy Buffett's most devoted and enthusiastic fans. It was a name that embodied the spirit of his music, evoking images of swaying palm trees, tropical cocktails, and the sense of belonging to a carefree tribe. The Parrothead community was more than just a fan base; it was a cultural movement, a lifestyle, and a family united by a shared love for Jimmy's music and the philosophy it espoused.

The genesis of the Parrothead phenomenon can be traced back to the vibrant atmosphere of Jimmy's live concerts. As he crisscrossed the country, performing in venues large and small, his shows took on a life of their own. Audiences didn't just attend his concerts; they participated in a communal experience, where music, camaraderie, and the Margaritaville ethos merged into something magical.

At Jimmy's concerts, fans would don Hawaiian shirts, leis, and straw hats, creating a sea of tropical attire in the audience. Beach balls would bounce through the crowd, and fans would raise their margaritas high in the air as they sang along to every word. It was a celebration of life, a temporary escape from the demands of the everyday world, and a reminder to savor the moment.

The Parrotheads weren't just spectators; they were active participants in the festivities. Tailgating parties in the parking lots before the shows became legendary, with fans setting up grills, blending margaritas, and sharing stories of their own adventures in pursuit of the Margaritaville lifestyle. These pre-concert gatherings were more than just warm-up events; they were a testament to the sense of community that bound the Parrothead tribe together.

As the Parrothead phenomenon gained momentum, it extended beyond the concert venues. Parrothead clubs sprang up across the country, forming a network of like-minded individuals who shared not only a passion for Jimmy's music but also a commitment to giving back to their communities. Parrothead clubs engaged in charitable activities, organizing fundraisers, beach cleanups, and other community service initiatives—a reflection of the values of environmental stewardship and social responsibility that were integral to Jimmy's music.

The Parrothead community also embraced the Margaritaville lifestyle in their everyday lives. They adopted the carefree spirit of Jimmy's songs, turning their homes into mini-tropical paradises, complete with tiki bars, palm trees, and beach decor. For Parrotheads, it wasn't just about attending concerts; it was about living the philosophy of Margaritaville—a life where worries were left behind, and every day was a vacation.

Jimmy Buffett himself welcomed the emergence of the Parrothead community with open arms. He recognized that his fans were more than just consumers of his music; they were partners in a shared journey. He affectionately referred to them as his "coral reefers," a nod to his band, the Coral Reefer Band, and the sense of camaraderie they all shared.

The Parrotheads became an integral part of Jimmy's career, and he made it a point to connect with them on a personal level. He interacted with fans, attended Parrothead club events, and even included their input in his creative endeavors. The Parrothead community was not just an audience; it was an extended family, and Jimmy Buffett was its patriarch.

As the 1980s gave way to the 1990s, the Parrothead phenomenon continued to grow, evolving into a cultural force that transcended music. It was a testament to the enduring appeal of Jimmy's music and the timeless message of his songs—a message that celebrated the pursuit of happiness, the magic of the Gulf Coast, and the joy of living life to the fullest.

The birth of the Parrothead community was a pivotal moment in the journey of Jimmy Buffett—a moment when his music became a catalyst for a lifestyle, a philosophy, and a sense of belonging. The Parrotheads were more than just fans; they were the living embodiment of the Margaritaville dream, and they would follow Jimmy on a musical odyssey that would span generations and continue to celebrate the endless summer of life by the sea.

4.2. Margaritaville: Restaurants, Resorts, and More

As the Parrothead community continued to flourish and Jimmy Buffett's music remained a soundtrack for a carefree lifestyle, a new chapter in the Margaritaville story was unfolding—one that would see the transformation of his music into a global brand, complete with restaurants, resorts, and a wide array of merchandise.

It was the early 2000s when Jimmy and his team decided to expand the Margaritaville experience beyond the concert stage. The idea was simple yet brilliant: to create physical spaces where fans could immerse themselves in the Margaritaville lifestyle year-round. And so began the journey of Margaritaville-branded restaurants and resorts.

The first Margaritaville restaurant opened its doors in Key West, Florida, in 1987. It was a natural choice for the flagship location, given the deep connection between Jimmy and the island. The restaurant, with its casual, beachy vibe, served up not only delicious food and drinks but also a healthy dose of Margaritaville ambiance. Visitors could dine on seafood, sip on frozen margaritas, and listen to Jimmy's music in the background—all while gazing at the turquoise waters of the Gulf of Mexico.

The Key West Margaritaville quickly became a beloved destination, attracting both tourists and locals who were eager to embrace the Margaritaville lifestyle. It was a place where time seemed to slow down, where every day was a vacation, and where the worries of the world faded away. The success of the Key West location laid the groundwork for what would become a global phenomenon.

Margaritaville restaurants began to spring up in cities across the United States and beyond. Each location retained the essence of the original—bright colors, tropical decor, and a menu filled with coastal-inspired cuisine. The restaurants weren't just places to eat; they were destinations in their own right, offering a taste of the Margaritaville experience to anyone who walked through their doors.

But Jimmy Buffett's vision extended beyond the dining table. He wanted to provide fans with the opportunity to fully immerse themselves in the Margaritaville lifestyle, and that meant offering places to stay that captured the spirit of his music. Thus, Margaritaville resorts were born.

The first Margaritaville resort opened in 2010 in Pensacola Beach, Florida. It was a beachfront paradise, complete with waterfront views, tiki bars, and a laid-back atmosphere. Guests could relax by the pool, enjoy live music, and savor the flavors of Margaritaville cuisine without ever leaving the property. The resort embodied the idea that a vacation could be more than just a destination; it could be an experience.

Margaritaville resorts continued to expand, with locations in destinations ranging from the Caribbean to the Smoky Mountains. Each resort offered a unique blend of luxury and relaxation, where guests could escape the stresses of everyday life and indulge in the Margaritaville lifestyle. It wasn't just a place to stay; it was a place to unwind, recharge, and embrace the magic of the Gulf Coast dream.

In addition to restaurants and resorts, the Margaritaville brand extended to a wide array of merchandise, from clothing and accessories to home decor and kitchenware. Fans could deck themselves out in Hawaiian shirts, Margaritaville flip-flops, and beach hats, creating a wardrobe that celebrated the carefree spirit of Jimmy's music. The brand allowed fans to bring a piece of Margaritaville into their everyday lives, whether they were at home or on vacation.

The expansion of the Margaritaville brand wasn't just a business venture; it was an extension of Jimmy's music and his philosophy of living life to the fullest. It was a way to share the magic of the Gulf Coast, the joy of escape, and the pursuit of happiness with fans around the world. The Margaritaville brand became a cultural touchstone, a symbol of the Margaritaville dream, and a testament to the enduring appeal of Jimmy Buffett's music.

As the Margaritaville empire continued to grow, Jimmy remained at the helm, guiding the brand with his trademark wit and wisdom. He continued to tour, perform, and connect with fans who had become part of the Margaritaville family. The restaurants, resorts, and merchandise were not just business endeavors; they were an extension of his music—a way to bring the Margaritaville lifestyle to life.

The Margaritaville phenomenon was not just a brand; it was a state of mind, a celebration of the Gulf Coast spirit, and a reminder to savor life's simple pleasures. It was a testament to the enduring appeal of Jimmy Buffett's music, which had transcended generations and continued to inspire a sense of escape, adventure, and the magic of the sea. As we continue to explore the chapters of Jimmy's life and music, the Margaritaville brand will remain a symbol of the endless summer—a reminder that in Margaritaville, every day is a beach day.

4.3. The Jimmy Buffett Brand

As the Margaritaville brand continued to flourish, it became more than just a collection of restaurants, resorts, and merchandise; it became synonymous with a lifestyle—a philosophy of living life to the fullest, embracing the Gulf Coast spirit, and savoring the moment. This lifestyle was personified by its creator, Jimmy Buffett, and it extended far beyond the boundaries of his music.

Jimmy Buffett had become more than a musician; he was a cultural icon, an ambassador of the good life, and a symbol of the Margaritaville dream. His brand wasn't built on flashy marketing campaigns or corporate strategies; it was built on authenticity, a deep connection with his fans, and a genuine love for the music and the lifestyle it celebrated.

At the heart of the Jimmy Buffett brand was the music itself—the songs that had captured the imaginations of fans for decades. His music was more than just a soundtrack; it was a reflection of his own experiences, his love for the Gulf Coast, and his unwavering commitment to the stories he wanted to share.

The songs were a source of comfort and inspiration for listeners of all ages. Whether it was the timeless allure of "Margaritaville," the reflective wisdom of "A Pirate Looks at Forty," or the bittersweet nostalgia of "Come Monday," Jimmy's lyrics spoke to the universal experiences of longing, adventure, and the pursuit of happiness.

But the brand wasn't just about the music; it was about the community of fans who had embraced the Margaritaville way of life. The Parrotheads, as they were affectionately known, were more than just fans; they were a tribe of like-minded individuals who shared not only a love for Jimmy's music but also a commitment to the values it embodied.

The Parrothead community was a testament to the power of music to unite people, transcend boundaries, and create a sense of belonging. They weren't just spectators; they were active participants in the Margaritaville experience, from tailgating parties before concerts to charitable initiatives that gave back to their communities. They embodied the spirit of the Gulf Coast dream, living it out in their everyday lives.

Jimmy Buffett himself was the living embodiment of the brand. He embraced the Margaritaville philosophy with gusto, from his laid-back demeanor and trademark Hawaiian shirts to his love for sailing, fishing, and the open sea. He was more than just a performer; he was a storyteller, a troubadour, and a captain of his own ship, both literally and figuratively.

His authenticity endeared him to fans and allowed him to connect with them on a personal level. He wasn't a distant celebrity; he was a friend, a mentor, and a kindred spirit. He interacted with fans, attended Parrothead club events, and made it a point to stay true to his roots and his values.

The Jimmy Buffett brand extended beyond music and community to encompass a wide array of ventures. His restaurants offered a taste of the Margaritaville lifestyle, his resorts provided a place to escape and unwind, and his merchandise allowed fans to bring a piece of Margaritaville into their everyday lives. Each element of the brand was an invitation to embrace the philosophy of Margaritaville—a life where worries were left behind, and every day was a vacation.

But perhaps the most enduring legacy of the Jimmy Buffett brand was its ability to inspire a sense of wanderlust and adventure. It encouraged fans to seek out their own "Margaritaville," whether it was on a remote island, a bustling city street, or a cozy corner of their own backyard. It reminded people that the pursuit of happiness wasn't confined to a specific place or time; it was a state of mind that could be embraced wherever one found themselves.

As we navigate the chapters of Jimmy Buffett's life and music, the Jimmy Buffett brand remains a symbol of the endless summer—a reminder that in Margaritaville, every day is a beach day, and every night is a party under the stars. It is a brand built on the enduring power of music, the magic of the Gulf Coast, and the joy of living life to the fullest—a brand that continues to inspire, unite, and celebrate the carefree spirit of the sea.

Chapter 5: Hits, Misses, and Comebacks

5.1. Notable Albums and Songs

As the decades rolled on, Jimmy Buffett's musical journey continued to be a kaleidoscope of hits, misses, and triumphant comebacks. His discography was a reflection of the ever-evolving Margaritaville sound, a tapestry woven with threads of folk, country, rock, and tropical rhythms. Here, we delve into some of the most notable albums and songs that defined this era of his career.

"Volcano" (1979): Released in the wake of the massive success of "Changes in Latitudes, Changes in Attitudes," "Volcano" kept the Margaritaville momentum going strong. The title track, with its infectious rhythm and vivid lyrics, beckoned listeners to the tropical paradise of St. Somewhere, where volcanoes rumbled and cocktails flowed. It was an album that captured the spirit of adventure, the allure of exotic destinations, and the joys of island escapism.

"Son of a Son of a Sailor" (1978): Building on the success of "Volcano," this album featured one of Jimmy's most enduring hits, "Cheeseburger in Paradise." The song celebrated life's simple pleasures—a juicy burger, a cold beer, and the company of good friends. It struck a chord with fans who found solace in its message of embracing the everyday joys of existence. The album itself was a nautical journey, with songs like "Son of a Son of a Sailor" and "Fool Button" evoking the romance of the open sea.

"One Particular Harbour" (1983): With its breezy melodies and tropical vibes, this album was a return to Jimmy's maritime roots. The title track, "One Particular Harbour," was a love letter to the islands, a place where dreams could take flight on the wings of a seagull. The album's themes of wanderlust, romance, and the search for meaning resonated with fans, and it remains a beloved classic in the Margaritaville catalog.

"License to Chill" (2004): This album marked a significant milestone in Jimmy's career, as it featured collaborations with a roster of musical legends, including Alan Jackson, George Strait, and Kenny Chesney. The album's title track, a duet with Kenny Chesney, became a chart-topping hit and introduced Jimmy's music to a new generation of country music fans. It was a testament to the enduring appeal of his music and its ability to transcend genres.

"Songs You Know by Heart" (1985): Often referred to as Jimmy's greatest hits album, "Songs You Know by Heart" was a compilation of his most beloved songs up to that point. It served as a musical roadmap of Jimmy's career, a collection of anthems that had become timeless classics. From "Margaritaville" to "A Pirate Looks at Forty," the album was a celebration of the stories and characters that had come to define the Margaritaville ethos.

These albums and songs were not just musical milestones; they were snapshots of the Margaritaville journey. They captured the essence of escape, the magic of the Gulf Coast, and the celebration of life's simple pleasures. While some albums soared to chart-topping heights, others became cult classics among devoted fans. But all of them were a testament to Jimmy Buffett's enduring talent as a storyteller, troubadour, and ambassador of the endless summer—a journey we will continue to explore as we navigate the highs and lows of his musical odyssey.

5.2. Career Highs and Lows

Jimmy Buffett's career was a rollercoaster ride of highs and lows, marked by chart-topping successes and moments of creative exploration. In this section, we delve into some of the pivotal moments that shaped his musical journey.

One of the career highs during this era was the release of "Floridays" in 1986. The album's title track was a poignant reflection on the passage of time and the desire to hold onto the moments that truly matter. "Floridays" showcased Jimmy's gift for storytelling, as he wove tales of love, nostalgia, and the beauty of the Florida Keys into his songs. The album resonated with fans, capturing the essence of the Margaritaville dream and earning its place as a cherished classic in Jimmy's discography.

However, the road to success was not without its challenges. The late 1980s and early 1990s saw a shift in the music industry, with changing tastes and trends. Jimmy faced the reality of evolving musical landscapes and shifting audience demographics. While some of his albums during this period received critical acclaim, they didn't always achieve the commercial success he had previously enjoyed.

Despite the occasional commercial setback, Jimmy remained true to his artistic vision. He continued to tour tirelessly, performing for packed audiences of loyal fans who had embraced the Margaritaville lifestyle. His live shows were a testament to his enduring appeal, as fans of all ages flocked to his concerts to bask in the glow of his music and the spirit of togetherness.

One of the most notable career lows during this period was the critical reception of the album "Last Mango in Paris" in 1985. While the album featured songs that would become fan favorites, such as "If the Phone Doesn't Ring, It's Me" and "First Look," it received mixed reviews from music critics. It was a reminder that even artists of Jimmy's stature were not immune to the ebb and flow of public and critical opinion.

However, Jimmy's resilience and dedication to his craft carried him through these challenging moments. He continued to release albums that explored new musical territories, from the bluesy "Riddles in the Sand" to the introspective "Fruitcakes." While these albums may not have achieved the same commercial success as some of his earlier work, they showcased his willingness to take creative risks and push the boundaries of his music.

One of the most notable career comebacks occurred in 2003 with the release of "License to Chill." The album featured collaborations with country music stars and marked a return to the top of the charts for Jimmy. The duet with Kenny Chesney on the title track was a chart-topping hit, introducing his music to a new generation of fans. It was a reminder that Jimmy's music had a timeless quality that could bridge genres and generations.

The highs and lows of Jimmy Buffett's career were a reflection of the ever-changing landscape of the music industry. Through it all, he remained a storyteller, a troubadour, and a captain of his own musical ship. His music continued to inspire a sense of escape, adventure, and the magic of the Gulf Coast—a journey we will continue to explore as we navigate the chapters of his life and music.

5.3. Reinvention and Ongoing Success

As the years rolled on and the Margaritaville legend continued to evolve, Jimmy Buffett found himself at a crossroads—a juncture that would ultimately lead to a reinvention of his music, brand, and legacy.

In the late 1990s and early 2000s, Jimmy faced the challenge of staying relevant in an ever-changing music industry. The landscape had shifted, with new genres and digital platforms reshaping how music was created, distributed, and consumed. Yet, Jimmy's commitment to his craft and his connection with fans remained unwavering.

It was during this period that Jimmy embraced a spirit of reinvention. He explored new musical horizons, blending his signature Margaritaville sound with elements of country, pop, and folk. This musical evolution was evident in albums like "Banana Wind" (1996) and "Don't Stop the Carnival" (1998). These albums showcased his versatility as an artist and his willingness to push the boundaries of his music.

But it wasn't just his music that underwent a transformation; it was also his approach to connecting with fans. Jimmy recognized the power of the internet as a tool for building and nurturing his community of Parrotheads. He launched a website, Margaritaville.com, which became a hub for fans to connect, share stories, and stay updated on all things Margaritaville.

Jimmy's live performances continued to be a cornerstone of his career, and he took his shows to new heights. His annual summer tours became a rite of passage for fans, a chance to gather under the open sky and celebrate the Margaritaville way of life. His concerts were more than just music; they were experiences, complete with tailgating parties, elaborate stage setups, and surprise guest appearances.

One of the defining moments of this era was the release of "Take the Weather with You" in 2006. The album featured a mix of original songs and cover tracks, including a heartfelt rendition of the John Hiatt song "What's New Pussycat?" Jimmy's collaboration with renowned musicians such as Mark Knopfler and Clint Black showcased his ability to bridge genres and create music that transcended boundaries.

The album's success was a testament to Jimmy's enduring appeal and his ability to stay relevant in an ever-changing music industry. It was also a reflection of the deep connection he maintained with his fans, who continued to flock to his concerts and embrace the Margaritaville lifestyle.

In addition to his music, Jimmy expanded his creative horizons into writing, publishing a series of novels and memoirs that further endeared him to his fans. His books, including "A Pirate Looks at Fifty" and "Tales from Margaritaville," offered readers a glimpse into his adventures, musings, and the stories that had shaped his life.

The ongoing success of Jimmy Buffett's career was not just about music; it was about a lifestyle—a philosophy of living life to the fullest, embracing the Gulf Coast spirit, and savoring the moment. His brand continued to thrive, with Margaritaville restaurants, resorts, merchandise, and a growing presence in the entertainment industry.

As we navigate the chapters of Jimmy's life and music, his journey of reinvention and ongoing success stands as a testament to his resilience, creativity, and unwavering commitment to the

Margaritaville dream. It is a journey that continues to inspire a sense of escape, adventure, and the magic of the Gulf Coast—a journey that invites us all to raise a glass, sing along, and celebrate the endless summer of life by the sea.

Chapter 6: Beyond Music

6.1. Literary Pursuits: Novels and Autobiography

In the rich tapestry of Jimmy Buffett's creative journey, his foray into the world of literature stands as a compelling narrative in its own right. Beyond the melodies and the margaritas, Jimmy proved himself to be a gifted storyteller in the realm of prose, penning a series of novels and memoirs that would transport readers to the same sun-soaked, salt-tinged world his songs had long evoked.

It was in 1989 that Jimmy Buffett's literary journey took its first steps with the publication of "Tales from Margaritaville." This collection of short stories was a delightful excursion into the whimsical, often humorous, and always entertaining world that had become synonymous with his music. The stories danced between the realms of fiction and reality, offering readers a glimpse into the characters, escapades, and colorful locales that had inspired his songs. From a fictional pirate named Tully Mars to a road trip down the Florida Keys, "Tales from Margaritaville" was a literary extension of Jimmy's music—a collection of tales that celebrated the pursuit of paradise.

However, it was with "A Pirate Looks at Fifty" that Jimmy Buffett's storytelling prowess truly came into its own. Published in 1998, this memoir was a reflection on his own journey through life, a candid exploration of his adventures, misadventures, and the wisdom he had gleaned along the way. The book was a literary voyage that took readers from the Gulf Coast to the Caribbean, from encounters with Hemingway's ghost to the perils of navigating the high seas. "A Pirate Looks at Fifty" was more than just a memoir; it was a testament to the spirit of wanderlust, the allure of the unknown, and the timeless quest for meaning.

Jimmy's literary pursuits continued with "Where Is Joe Merchant?" (1992) and "Don't Stop the Carnival" (1998), both novels that blended his storytelling with elements of escapism, humor, and the pursuit of dreams. "Where Is Joe Merchant?" was a globe-trotting adventure filled with eccentric characters, exotic locales, and the ever-present siren call of the sea. It was a novel that captured the essence of Jimmy's own wanderlust and his love for the open ocean.

Meanwhile, "Don't Stop the Carnival" was a fictional tale set in the Caribbean, exploring the escapades of a protagonist who buys a run-down hotel on a tropical island. The novel was a blend of comedy and drama, a reflection on the challenges and rewards of pursuing one's dreams in a far-flung paradise. It resonated with readers who shared Jimmy's own passion for the islands and the promise of a carefree existence.

Jimmy's literary pursuits were not simply a creative side project; they were an extension of his storytelling legacy. Just as his songs had painted vivid pictures of a life by the sea, his books transported readers to the same sun-drenched shores, where the music played, the cocktails flowed, and the worries of the world faded away. His literary works celebrated the spirit of adventure, the magic of the Gulf Coast, and the pursuit of happiness—a journey we will continue to explore as we navigate the chapters of his life and creativity.

6.2. Acting and Appearances in Film and Television

Jimmy Buffett's creative journey extended far beyond the confines of the concert stage and recording studio. He ventured into the world of film and television, where his charismatic presence and love for storytelling found new avenues of expression.

One of his earliest forays into acting was a cameo appearance in the 1975 film "Rancho Deluxe." In this offbeat Western comedy, Jimmy played the role of a singing cowboy, and his brief but memorable appearance showcased his knack for injecting humor and charm into any role. It was a taste of things to come, hinting at his potential as a performer in the visual medium.

However, it was in the 1980 film "Urban Cowboy" that Jimmy Buffett made a more significant mark on the silver screen. He portrayed the character of a barman named "Charlie," a role that allowed him to bring his signature laid-back charm to the big screen. The film was a celebration of country music and the Texas honky-tonk culture, and Jimmy's presence added an authentic touch to the film's ambiance.

Television also became a platform for Jimmy's creative talents. He made appearances on popular shows such as "Saturday Night Live" and "The Tonight Show Starring Johnny Carson," where he showcased his wit, humor, and musical talents. These television appearances solidified his status as a beloved entertainer beyond the music world.

One of the most notable moments in Jimmy's television career was his recurring role on the hit show "Hawaii Five-O" in the 2010s. He played the character of Frank Bama, a helicopter pilot and friend to the show's main characters. It was a role that allowed him to embrace his love for flying and the allure of the Hawaiian islands. His appearances on the show brought his character to life, and fans eagerly anticipated each episode in which he appeared.

Beyond acting, Jimmy Buffett also lent his voice to various animated films and television series. His distinctive voice was a natural fit for animated characters, and his roles in projects like "The Simpsons" and "South Park" showcased his ability to infuse humor and personality into his voice acting.

Throughout his ventures in film and television, Jimmy Buffett remained true to his persona—a charismatic, easygoing storyteller who had a knack for connecting with audiences. Whether on the big screen or the small screen, his appearances were a testament to his versatility as an entertainer and his enduring appeal as a cultural icon.

These forays into film and television were not mere diversions from his music career; they were extensions of his storytelling legacy. They allowed him to reach new audiences, showcase his talents in different ways, and add depth to the characters and narratives he encountered. Just as his songs had painted vivid pictures of life by the sea, his appearances in film and television added new dimensions to the Margaritaville legend—a journey we will continue to explore as we navigate the chapters of his life and creativity.

6.3. Philanthropy and Environmental Advocacy

As Jimmy Buffett's career soared to new heights, he recognized the importance of using his influence and resources to make a positive impact on the world. Beyond the stage and the recording studio, he embarked on a journey of philanthropy and environmental advocacy that would become an integral part of his legacy.

One of the causes closest to Jimmy's heart was environmental conservation. His love for the Gulf Coast and the Caribbean islands had instilled in him a deep sense of responsibility to protect these natural treasures. In the wake of the devastating Deepwater Horizon oil spill in 2010, Jimmy took action. He co-founded the Gulf Coast Conservation Initiative, a nonprofit organization dedicated to the long-term recovery and preservation of the Gulf of Mexico.

Through the initiative, Jimmy used his voice and platform to raise awareness about the environmental challenges facing the Gulf Coast. He advocated for responsible stewardship of the region's delicate ecosystems and worked tirelessly to ensure that the Gulf's vibrant marine life, pristine beaches, and unique culture would be preserved for future generations.

In addition to his efforts in the Gulf Coast, Jimmy was a vocal advocate for coral reef conservation. His love for snorkeling and diving had led him to witness the beauty and fragility of coral reefs around the world. He supported organizations such as The Nature Conservancy in their efforts to protect and restore these vital marine ecosystems.

But Jimmy's philanthropic endeavors extended beyond environmental causes. He was a strong supporter of charitable initiatives that focused on education, healthcare, and disaster relief. He used his annual tours as opportunities to give back to the communities he visited, often donating a portion of concert proceeds to local charities and organizations.

One of the most enduring legacies of Jimmy's philanthropy was the creation of the Singing for Change charitable foundation. Established in 1995, the foundation aimed to support a wide range of social and environmental causes. It provided grants to organizations working on issues such as education, poverty alleviation, and environmental conservation.

Jimmy's commitment to philanthropy was not just about writing checks; it was about using his platform and influence to effect positive change. He leveraged his celebrity status to shine a spotlight on pressing issues, whether it was advocating for renewable energy solutions or supporting disaster relief efforts in the aftermath of hurricanes and natural disasters.

His philanthropic journey was a testament to his belief in the power of individuals to make a difference. He encouraged his fans, known as Parrotheads, to get involved in charitable initiatives and give back to their communities. He believed that the Margaritaville way of life was not just about escapism; it was also about embracing a spirit of compassion and making the world a better place.

As we navigate the chapters of Jimmy Buffett's life and creativity, his legacy of philanthropy and environmental advocacy stands as a reminder that music can be a force for positive change. It is a legacy that inspires us to take action, protect the natural world, and embrace a spirit of giving—a journey that invites us all to raise a glass, sing along, and make the world a little more like Margaritaville.

Chapter 7: Personal Life

7.1. Marriages, Relationships, and Family

In the midst of Jimmy Buffett's whirlwind career and the Margaritaville lifestyle he championed, his personal life was a rich tapestry woven with relationships, marriages, and the bonds of family. It was a dimension of his life that added depth to the troubadour of the sea.

Jimmy's journey through the realm of romance and relationships was as colorful as the characters that populated his songs. His first marriage was to Margie Washichek, and together they had two children, a son named Savannah Jane and a daughter named Sarah Delaney. However, as his music career gained momentum, the demands of life on the road took a toll on their marriage, and they eventually divorced.

Yet, it was during this period that Jimmy's music was also marked by themes of love, heartache, and the complexities of human relationships. Songs like "Come Monday" and "Changes in Latitudes, Changes in Attitudes" resonated with listeners who had experienced the ebb and flow of love's tides.

Jimmy's personal life took a turn when he met and fell in love with Jane Slagsvol. Their love story would become the inspiration for the hit song "Jane," a tribute to the woman who had captured his heart. Their relationship would go on to become a lasting partnership marked by mutual support and a shared love for the Margaritaville dream.

In 1977, Jimmy and Jane tied the knot in a private ceremony, and their union brought stability and companionship to Jimmy's life. Together, they welcomed two children into their family, a son named Cameron Marley and a daughter named Isabella. The Buffett family, with its blend of children from previous marriages and their own, embodied the spirit of togetherness and celebration that was at the core of the Margaritaville lifestyle.

Throughout the years, Jimmy's family played a significant role in his life and career. They became his anchor, his source of inspiration, and a reminder of the importance of balancing the demands of the road with the joys of home. His children would grow up immersed in the world of music, adventure, and the magic of the Gulf Coast, often joining their father on tour and experiencing the thrill of performing for adoring crowds.

As the years rolled on, Jimmy's family continued to be a central part of his life. They celebrated milestones together, shared the ups and downs of life, and embraced the Margaritaville way of living. Jimmy's personal journey, marked by marriages, relationships, and the bonds of family, added a layer of authenticity to his music. His songs were not just stories from a distant shore; they were reflections of the experiences, joys, and challenges of a life well-lived.

7.2. Hobbies and Interests: Sailing, Flying, and More

Beyond the spotlight and the music, Jimmy Buffett's personal life was a tapestry woven with passions, hobbies, and adventures that mirrored the themes of escapism and exploration found in his songs. His love for the sea, the open sky, and the great outdoors became defining elements of his identity.

One of Jimmy's enduring passions was sailing. From his early days growing up along the Gulf Coast to his later adventures in the Caribbean, the call of the sea was a constant in his life. He was drawn to the freedom and serenity of sailing, and his experiences on the water would inspire some of his most iconic songs. The sea became both muse and mentor, shaping his music and his outlook on life.

Jimmy's love for sailing extended to his own vessels, including a series of sailboats that bore the name "Euphoria." These boats became his floating sanctuaries, offering him a respite from the demands of his music career and a canvas on which to create new adventures. Whether it was cruising the Florida Keys, exploring the islands of the Caribbean, or embarking on transatlantic crossings, sailing allowed him to embrace the Margaritaville dream of living life at a leisurely pace.

Another passion that soared alongside Jimmy's music career was his love for flying. He held a pilot's license and often took to the skies in his own aircraft. Flying allowed him to combine his adventurous spirit with his wanderlust, exploring new destinations and experiencing the thrill of soaring above the clouds. His adventures in the air became a source of inspiration for songs like "Wings" and "Presents to Send You."

Jimmy's hobbies and interests were not limited to the sea and the sky; they also extended to the culinary world. He was known for his love of cooking and a fondness for experimenting with recipes. This passion for food and drink found expression in his Margaritaville restaurants, where patrons could savor dishes inspired by his travels and experiences.

His hobbies and interests were not just personal indulgences; they became integral aspects of the Margaritaville brand. His love for sailing, flying, and culinary delights was woven into the fabric of the Margaritaville lifestyle, inviting fans to share in the same sense of adventure and enjoyment. His songs, concerts, and ventures all reflected his deep connection to these passions, creating a sense of camaraderie among fans who shared in the dream of escape and exploration.

In navigating the chapters of Jimmy Buffett's personal life, we discover the rich tapestry of his interests and pursuits. From the sea to the sky, from the kitchen to the concert stage, his hobbies became more than pastimes; they were reflections of a life lived to the fullest. They were an invitation to embrace the Margaritaville way of life—a journey where every day was a vacation and every moment was a celebration of the endless summer.

7.3. Challenges and Triumphs in Personal Life

Amid the sun-soaked shores and harmonious melodies of Jimmy Buffett's life, there were moments of both challenge and triumph that added depth to his personal journey.

One of the most significant challenges in Jimmy's life was a near-fatal accident in 1996. While on a hike in Nantucket, he fell off a stage, suffering a serious head injury. The accident left him in a coma and required extensive rehabilitation. It was a moment that brought his life to a halt, forcing him to confront mortality and the fragility of the human experience.

But true to his resilient spirit, Jimmy emerged from this ordeal with a renewed sense of purpose. He channeled his determination into his recovery, working tirelessly to regain his strength and vitality. The experience deepened his appreciation for life's precious moments and became a source of inspiration for songs like "Breathe In, Breathe Out, Move On." It was a reminder that even in the face of adversity, the Margaritaville way of life—a philosophy of savoring the present—remained steadfast.

Triumphs in Jimmy's personal life were intertwined with his creative journey. His family, his passions, and his sense of adventure were sources of joy and fulfillment. The enduring love and support of his wife, Jane, and the bonds he shared with his children and extended family were constants in his life. These relationships were a testament to the strength of the Margaritaville ethos—a celebration of love, togetherness, and the pursuit of happiness.

Another personal triumph for Jimmy was the establishment of the Margaritaville brand, which expanded from music into restaurants, resorts, merchandise, and entertainment ventures. The Margaritaville lifestyle became a cultural phenomenon, inviting fans to embrace a carefree, island-inspired way of life. It was a testament to Jimmy's ability to create a brand that resonated with people around the world and a reminder that dreams could become reality.

Jimmy's personal journey was also marked by his philanthropic and environmental advocacy efforts, where he used his influence to make a positive impact on the world. His dedication to causes like Gulf Coast conservation and coral reef protection showcased his commitment to leaving a lasting legacy beyond the music.

As we navigate the chapters of Jimmy Buffett's personal life, we encounter the challenges that tested his resilience and the triumphs that celebrated his unwavering spirit. His journey was a reminder that even in the Margaritaville of life, where the sun always shines and the music never stops, there were moments of darkness and moments of light. It was a journey that invited us all to raise a glass, sing along, and embrace the full spectrum of the human experience—a journey that celebrated the endless summer by the sea.

Chapter 8: The Legacy of Jimmy Buffett

8.1. Influence on Music and Culture

Jimmy Buffett's influence on music and culture was akin to the gentle sway of a hammock on a sun-drenched beach—soothing, infectious, and impossible to resist. His journey from a young troubadour strumming a guitar in Key West to an iconic figure of island escapism left an indelible mark on both the musical landscape and the collective imagination.

In the realm of music, Jimmy's contributions were nothing short of groundbreaking. He pioneered a genre that came to be known as "Gulf and Western," blending elements of folk, country, rock, and tropical rhythms to create a sound that was uniquely his own. His songs, infused with tales of pirates, sailors, and sun-soaked reverie, transported listeners to a world where worries drifted away with the tide. The Margaritaville sound became a soundtrack for carefree living, and his dedicated fanbase, known as Parrotheads, grew with each new release.

Key to Jimmy's musical allure was his gift for storytelling. His lyrics painted vivid pictures of life by the sea, with characters like Captain Tony, Tully Mars, and the mythical "Drunken Sailor" coming to life in his songs. He was a troubadour of the Gulf Coast, spinning tales of adventure, romance, and the search for paradise. His storytelling prowess extended to his novels and memoirs, further cementing his status as a masterful raconteur.

Beyond the music, Jimmy's cultural impact was felt in the lifestyle he embodied and celebrated—a lifestyle of flip-flops, beachfront bars, and the pursuit of the perfect margarita. He invited fans to escape the daily grind and embrace the Margaritaville way of life, a philosophy of slowing down, savoring the moment, and finding joy in simple pleasures. This ethos resonated with a wide range of people who craved an escape from the demands of modern life.

The Margaritaville brand, which expanded into restaurants, resorts, merchandise, and entertainment ventures, became a cultural phenomenon in its own right. Fans flocked to Margaritaville destinations around the world, seeking to experience the magic of a place where it was always 5 o'clock, and the party never stopped. The brand embodied the spirit of Jimmy's music and the idea that life was meant to be lived with a sense of adventure and spontaneity.

Jimmy's influence also extended to the world of philanthropy and environmental advocacy. He used his platform and resources to support causes he was passionate about, from Gulf Coast conservation to coral reef protection. His commitment to making a positive impact on the world mirrored the values of his music and the sense of responsibility to protect the natural treasures of the Gulf Coast.

As we navigate the chapters of Jimmy Buffett's legacy, we uncover a legacy of music and culture that transcends generations. He was more than a musician; he was a storyteller, a cultural icon, and a purveyor of the Margaritaville dream. His influence was not just about songs and stories; it was about inviting people to embrace a lifestyle of escape, adventure, and the endless summer by the sea—a legacy that continues to inspire, to celebrate, and to remind us to raise a glass, sing along, and live life to the fullest.

8.2. The Enduring Appeal of Margaritaville

In the world of entertainment and pop culture, where trends often come and go like passing waves, the Margaritaville brand created by Jimmy Buffett stands as a testament to enduring appeal. It's a brand that not only survived the test of time but thrived, inviting generations to embrace a carefree, island-inspired lifestyle.

At the heart of the Margaritaville phenomenon was a simple yet powerful philosophy—a philosophy that said it was okay to slow down, savor the moment, and find joy in life's simple pleasures. It was a philosophy that resonated with people of all ages and backgrounds, from college students seeking an escape to retirees longing for a life of leisure.

The Margaritaville lifestyle was about more than just music; it was a state of mind. It was about escaping the daily grind, even if just for a few hours, and immersing oneself in a world of flip-flops, beachfront bars, and the pursuit of the perfect margarita. It was a world where it was always 5 o'clock, where worries drifted away with the tide, and where the idea of "fins to the left, fins to the right" was a call to let loose and dance in the sand.

The enduring appeal of Margaritaville was evident in the brand's expansion into restaurants, resorts, merchandise, and even retirement communities. Margaritaville destinations sprang up in tropical locales, urban centers, and everywhere in between, offering fans a taste of the Margaritaville dream. From sipping margaritas at a Tiki bar to relaxing in a beachfront hammock, visitors could immerse themselves in the same world that Jimmy's songs had evoked for decades.

The Margaritaville brand became a cultural phenomenon in its own right, attracting not only Parrotheads but also a broader audience looking for an escape from the demands of modern life. It was a place where music played, the cocktails flowed, and the worries of the world faded into the background. It was a place that celebrated the idea that life was meant to be lived with a sense of adventure and spontaneity.

Part of Margaritaville's enduring appeal was its adaptability. It remained a relevant and relatable concept, evolving with the times while staying true to its core values. Jimmy's music continued to draw new fans, and the brand's expansion into merchandise and entertainment ventures provided multiple entry points into the Margaritaville world.

Perhaps most significantly, the Margaritaville brand was a celebration of the idea that age was just a number. It appealed to a diverse demographic, from college students dancing to "Cheeseburger in Paradise" to retirees embracing the Margaritaville lifestyle in their golden years. It was a reminder that the pursuit of happiness and the dream of paradise were timeless, ageless pursuits.

As we navigate the chapters of Jimmy Buffett's legacy, the enduring appeal of Margaritaville stands as a testament to the power of music, storytelling, and the pursuit of a dream. It is a reminder that even in a world of constant change, there are places and philosophies that remain timeless—a legacy that continues to inspire, to celebrate, and to remind us to raise a glass, sing along, and live life to the fullest, by the sea.

8.3. Honors, Awards, and Recognition

The sun-soaked melodies of Jimmy Buffett's music and the carefree spirit of Margaritaville resonated with millions around the world, and the recognition of his contributions to music, culture, and philanthropy was reflected in a host of honors and awards that celebrated his enduring legacy.

One of the most significant milestones in Jimmy's career was his induction into the Songwriters Hall of Fame in 2006. This prestigious honor recognized his songwriting prowess and the profound impact of his lyrics, which painted vivid pictures of life by the sea, love, and adventure. It was a testament to his ability to craft songs that transcended generations and captured the essence of the Margaritaville lifestyle.

In 2010, Jimmy received another remarkable accolade when he was presented with the CMA (Country Music Association) Humanitarian Award. This award recognized his philanthropic efforts and dedication to causes such as Gulf Coast conservation, coral reef protection, and disaster relief. It underscored his commitment to making a positive impact on the world beyond the realm of music.

Throughout his career, Jimmy was also the recipient of numerous Grammy nominations, reflecting the musical excellence that defined his work. While the elusive Grammy win remained just out of reach, his enduring popularity and influence within the music industry were undeniable.

Jimmy's contributions to popular culture extended beyond music and philanthropy. He made appearances in films and television, showcasing his charisma and storytelling prowess on the big and small screens. These endeavors earned him recognition from the entertainment industry and cemented his status as a multi-talented entertainer.

Perhaps one of the most heartfelt recognitions of Jimmy's legacy came from his dedicated fanbase, the Parrotheads. They celebrated his music, embraced the Margaritaville lifestyle, and formed a vibrant community of fans who reveled in the escapism and adventure he offered. Jimmy's concerts became annual pilgrimages for Parrotheads, who transformed arenas and amphitheaters into a sea of Hawaiian shirts, leis, and straw hats.

In 2020, Jimmy received a star on the Hollywood Walk of Fame, an honor that underscored his enduring impact on entertainment and culture. It was a recognition of the indelible mark he had left on the world of music, film, television, and philanthropy—a mark that extended far beyond the boundaries of the sidewalk.

Throughout his career, Jimmy Buffett's honors, awards, and recognition served as a reflection of the profound and enduring impact of his work. They celebrated not only his musical talent but also his storytelling prowess, his philanthropic endeavors, and his ability to create a cultural phenomenon that invited people to embrace a lifestyle of escape and celebration. These accolades were a testament to the power of the Margaritaville dream, a dream that continues to inspire, to celebrate, and to remind us to raise a glass, sing along, and live life to the fullest, by the sea.

Chapter 9: Looking Ahead

9.1. Current Projects and Future Plans

As the sun continues to set over the horizon of Jimmy Buffett's storied career, it casts a warm glow on a future filled with promise, creativity, and a commitment to the Margaritaville dream.

One of the most exciting aspects of Jimmy's current endeavors is his ongoing commitment to creating new music. Despite decades in the industry, he remains as passionate as ever about songwriting and performing. His deep well of inspiration, drawn from a lifetime of adventures and escapades, continues to yield fresh melodies and lyrics that capture the spirit of Margaritaville.

Jimmy's connection with his fans, affectionately known as Parrotheads, remains a driving force in his creative journey. His annual tours are a celebration of this dedicated community, and he shows no signs of slowing down. Each concert is an opportunity to transport audiences to the sun-soaked shores of Margaritaville, where they can leave their worries behind and embrace the carefree spirit of the music.

In addition to his music, Jimmy continues to expand the Margaritaville brand into new and exciting ventures. Margaritaville resorts and restaurants continue to thrive in locations around the world, offering fans and travelers alike a taste of the Margaritaville lifestyle. These destinations are more than just businesses; they are an extension of the Margaritaville dream—a place where it's always 5 o'clock, and the party never stops.

Jimmy's literary pursuits also continue to flourish. He has penned a series of novels and memoirs that transport readers to the same sun-soaked, salt-tinged world his songs have long evoked. His storytelling prowess remains as captivating as ever, and his fans eagerly anticipate each new literary adventure.

Beyond music and literature, Jimmy's commitment to philanthropy and environmental advocacy remains steadfast. His dedication to causes such as Gulf Coast conservation and coral reef protection continues to make a positive impact on the world. His influence and resources have the potential to effect change and inspire others to embrace a spirit of compassion and stewardship for the environment.

As we look ahead to the future chapters of Jimmy Buffett's career, we see a man who shows no signs of slowing down. His commitment to the Margaritaville dream, his dedication to his fans, and his ongoing creative endeavors are a testament to his enduring passion for music, storytelling, and the pursuit of happiness. The Margaritaville lifestyle, with its sunsets, flip-flops, and endless summer, remains a beacon of hope and a reminder to live life to the fullest. It invites us all to raise a glass, sing along, and embrace the promise of a future filled with laughter, adventure, and the sweet sound of steel drums by the sea.

9.2. The Jimmy Buffett Fan Community Today

The Jimmy Buffett fan community, affectionately known as the Parrotheads, stands as a vibrant and enduring testament to the power of music and the Margaritaville lifestyle. Today, this community continues to thrive, evolving with the times while staying true to the spirit of escapism, camaraderie, and celebration that has defined it for decades.

At the heart of the Parrothead community is a shared love for Jimmy's music and the Margaritaville ethos. It's a community that transcends age, background, and geographic boundaries, united by a common desire to escape the daily grind and embrace a carefree, island-inspired way of life. Parrotheads gather at Jimmy's concerts, transforming venues into a sea of Hawaiian shirts, leis, and straw hats. The tailgating parties that precede these shows are legendary, with fans creating elaborate setups featuring beach decor, grills, and an abundance of food and drinks. It's a joyful celebration of music and friendship, where strangers become fast friends under the banner of Margaritaville.

In the digital age, the Parrothead community has found new ways to connect and celebrate. Online forums, social media groups, and fan websites have become virtual gathering places where fans share stories, swap concert tips, and celebrate their shared love for Jimmy's music. These online communities have expanded the reach of the Parrothead community, connecting fans from around the world and providing a platform for them to share their own Margaritaville-inspired adventures.

The Parrothead community is not just about music; it's about a way of life. It's about embracing the philosophy of slowing down, savoring the moment, and finding joy in life's simple pleasures. It's about creating a sense of escapism, even if just for a few hours, and immersing oneself in a world where worries drift away with the tide. It's a community that believes in the power of music to transport, to heal, and to unite.

Jimmy Buffett's connection with his fan community remains as strong as ever. His annual tours are not just concerts; they are celebrations of the Parrothead spirit. He engages with his fans both on and off stage, sharing stories, raising a glass, and inviting them to be a part of the Margaritaville experience. His authenticity and accessibility have endeared him to fans, creating a unique bond that transcends the typical artist-fan relationship.

As the Parrothead community looks to the future, they do so with a sense of anticipation and excitement. They know that the Margaritaville dream, with its sunsets, flip-flops, and endless summer, is not just a fleeting fantasy; it's a way of life. It's a way of embracing the present, finding joy in the company of friends, and celebrating the magic of music. It's a community that understands that, no matter where they are, they can always find their way back to Margaritaville—a place where the music never stops, the drinks are always cold, and the party goes on forever.

9.3. The Endless Summer: Jimmy's Unwavering Spirit

As Jimmy Buffett continues to sail through the chapters of his storied career, one thing remains abundantly clear: his spirit is unwavering, his enthusiasm undiminished, and his commitment to the Margaritaville dream unshakable. The notion of an "endless summer" is not just a lyric in one of his songs; it's a philosophy that defines his approach to life.

Throughout his journey, Jimmy has encountered challenges, experienced setbacks, and weathered the storms of both life and the sea. Yet, his resilience and optimism have remained constant. His ability to find joy in the simplest of moments, to savor the present, and to inspire others to do the same is a testament to his unwavering spirit.

In the face of adversity, such as a near-fatal accident in 1996 that left him in a coma, Jimmy emerged not only as a survivor but as a symbol of perseverance. He channeled his determination into his recovery, using music as a source of healing and inspiration. His song "Breathe In, Breathe Out, Move On" became an anthem of resilience and a reminder that even in the darkest of times, there is a way forward.

Jimmy's unwavering spirit is also evident in his ongoing creative endeavors. His passion for songwriting, performing, and storytelling remains as fervent as ever. He continues to create new music, share new stories, and transport audiences to the sun-soaked shores of Margaritaville. His concerts are not just performances; they are celebrations of life, of music, and of the enduring spirit of escape and adventure.

The Margaritaville brand, with its restaurants, resorts, merchandise, and entertainment ventures, continues to expand and flourish under Jimmy's guidance. It's a brand that celebrates the idea that life is meant to be lived with a sense of spontaneity and joy. It's a brand that reminds us to embrace the present, to find happiness in the company of friends, and to savor every moment as if it were the sweetest of margaritas.

Perhaps most significantly, Jimmy's unwavering spirit is reflected in his commitment to philanthropy and environmental advocacy. His dedication to causes such as Gulf Coast conservation and coral reef protection showcases his belief in the power of individuals to effect positive change. He leverages his influence and resources to make a lasting impact on the world, embodying the Margaritaville ethos of giving back and protecting the natural treasures of the Gulf Coast.

Conclusion

10.1. Reflecting on the Parrothead Phenomenon

In the annals of music history, the name Jimmy Buffett stands as a beacon of sun-soaked melodies, carefree living, and the enduring power of storytelling. Through the pages of this biography, we have embarked on a journey—a journey that has taken us from the roots of a young troubadour in Mobile, Alabama, to the iconic figure of island escapism and the Margaritaville lifestyle that he embodies.

Jimmy's life story is one of adventure, resilience, and unwavering passion. From his childhood days along the Gulf Coast, where the sea and the sun became his constant companions, to his forays into music, literature, and philanthropy, his journey has been marked by a commitment to celebrating life, cherishing the present, and inviting others to do the same.

As we have navigated the chapters of this biography, we have explored the intricate tapestry of Jimmy's life—the family ties, the early influences, the breakthrough moments, and the enduring impact of his music and culture. We have delved into his personal life, his relationships, and the challenges and triumphs that have shaped him as both an artist and a man.

The legacy of Jimmy Buffett is not confined to the realm of music; it extends to a lifestyle, a philosophy, and a community. It is a legacy that invites us all to embrace the Margaritaville dream—a dream of escape, adventure, and the pursuit of happiness. It is a legacy that reminds us to raise a glass, sing along, and live life to the fullest, by the sea.

As we look to the future, we see a Jimmy Buffett who remains as vibrant and passionate as ever. His ongoing creative endeavors, his commitment to philanthropy and environmental advocacy, and his enduring connection with the Parrothead community are all testaments to a life well-lived and a spirit that refuses to be dimmed.

In closing, the story of Jimmy Buffett is a story of a man who transformed music, culture, and the way we view the world. It is a story of a troubadour who became an icon, a storyteller who became a legend, and a dreamer who invited us all to dream along with him. In the endless summer of Margaritaville, the sun always shines, the music never stops, and the party goes on forever. So, let us raise a glass one more time to Jimmy Buffett—a living legend who reminds us that life is a beach, and every day is a vacation.

10.2. Jimmy Buffett's Place in Music History

When we consider the tapestry of music history, we find that Jimmy Buffett occupies a unique and vibrant corner, where the sun always shines, and the rhythm is set to the gentle sway of a hammock. His place in music history is not defined by chart-topping hits or record-breaking album sales, but rather by the profound and enduring impact of his music on the hearts and souls of listeners around the world.

Jimmy Buffett's genre-defying sound, often referred to as "Gulf and Western," is a testament to his ability to blend elements of folk, country, rock, and tropical rhythms into a sound that is uniquely his own. His songs transport us to a world where worries are left behind, and we are invited to embrace the Margaritaville dream—a dream of escape, adventure, and the pursuit of happiness.

While the charts may not have always reflected the depth of his influence, Jimmy's music has transcended the boundaries of traditional success. His songs, infused with tales of pirates, sailors, and sun-soaked reverie, have become anthems of carefree living and celebration. They have been woven into the fabric of popular culture, earning him a dedicated and diverse fanbase that spans generations.

Jimmy's storytelling prowess is another hallmark of his place in music history. Through his lyrics, he has created vivid and enduring characters—Captain Tony, Tully Mars, and the mythical "Drunken Sailor," to name a few. His songs are not just compositions; they are tales of adventure, romance, and the search for paradise. They are stories that resonate with listeners, inviting them to step into the world he has crafted.

Beyond the music, Jimmy's influence extends to the Margaritaville brand—a lifestyle empire that includes restaurants, resorts, merchandise, and entertainment ventures. This brand has become a cultural phenomenon in its own right, inviting fans and travelers to immerse themselves in the Margaritaville dream. It is a brand that celebrates the philosophy of slowing down, savoring the moment, and finding joy in life's simple pleasures.

As we reflect on Jimmy Buffett's place in music history, we find that it is a place defined not only by the melodies he has created but also by the way he has invited us to live. It is a place where the sun always sets in shades of orange and pink, where flip-flops are the footwear of choice, and where the pursuit of happiness is a way of life. It is a place where music and storytelling have the power to transport us to a world of endless summer, and where the legacy of Jimmy Buffett continues to inspire, to celebrate, and to remind us to raise a glass, sing along, and live life to the fullest, by the sea.

10.3. Closing Thoughts and Final Insights

In the closing chords of this narrative, we find ourselves reflecting on the life and legacy of Jimmy Buffett—a troubadour, storyteller, and creator of the Margaritaville dream. His journey has been one of sunsets and steel drums, of resilience and unwavering spirit, and of music that has touched the hearts of millions.

Jimmy Buffett's legacy is a tapestry woven from the threads of his music, his storytelling prowess, and his unwavering commitment to celebrating life. It is a legacy that transcends the confines of traditional success and charts its course in the hearts of his dedicated fans—the Parrotheads who have embraced his music and his message with unwavering enthusiasm.

Through his genre-defying sound, Jimmy carved out a niche in music history that is uniquely his own. His songs, infused with tales of adventure and escape, have become anthems of carefree living. They invite us to leave our worries behind, even if just for a few minutes, and to embrace the Margaritaville way of life—a way of slowing down, savoring the moment, and finding joy in life's simple pleasures.

But Jimmy's legacy extends beyond music; it is a lifestyle, a philosophy, and a sense of community. The Margaritaville brand, with its restaurants, resorts, merchandise, and entertainment ventures, celebrates this way of life, inviting fans to immerse themselves in the dream. It is a brand that reflects the belief that life is meant to be lived with a sense of adventure and spontaneity, and it has become a cultural phenomenon that resonates with people around the world.

As we reflect on Jimmy Buffett's place in music history, we find that it is not just about the songs he has written or the albums he has recorded; it is about the way he has invited us to live. It is about embracing the philosophy of Margaritaville—a philosophy that says it's okay to escape, to celebrate, and to find happiness in the company of friends. It is a philosophy that reminds us that, no matter where we are, we can always find our way back to Margaritaville—a place where the music never stops, the drinks are always cold, and the party goes on forever.

In closing, the legacy of Jimmy Buffett is a reminder that, in the world of music and beyond, there are individuals whose impact goes beyond the charts and the accolades. They touch our lives in profound ways, inviting us to celebrate, to escape, and to savor the present. Jimmy Buffett is one such individual, a living legend who continues to inspire, to celebrate, and to remind us to raise a glass, sing along, and live life to the fullest, by the sea. His legacy is the promise of an endless summer—a promise that, in the Margaritaville of life, is as timeless as a song, as comforting as a hammock, and as enduring as the love for a life well-lived.

Appendices

A. Discography: Albums, Singles, and Collaborations

Albums:

- Down to Earth (1970)
- High Cumberland Jubilee (1971)
- A White Sport Coat and a Pink Crustacean (1973)
- Living and Dying in 3/4 Time (1974)
- A1A (1974)
- Havana Daydreamin' (1976)
- Changes in Latitudes, Changes in Attitudes (1977)
- Son of a Son of a Sailor (1978)
- Volcano (1979)
- Coconut Telegraph (1981)
- Somewhere over China (1982)
- One Particular Harbour (1983)
- Riddles in the Sand (1984)
- Last Mango in Paris (1985)
- Floridays (1986)
- Hot Water (1988)
- Off to See the Lizard (1989)
- Feeding Frenzy: Live (1990)
- Christmas Island (1996)
- Barometer Soup (1995)
- Banana Wind (1996)
- Don't Stop the Carnival (1998)
- Beach House on the Moon (1999)
- Far Side of the World (2002)

- License to Chill (2004)
- Take the Weather with You (2006)
- Buffet Hotel (2009)
- Encores (2010)
- Songs from St. Somewhere (2013)
- Tis the SeaSon (2016)
- Life on the Flip Side (2020)

Singles:

- "Margaritaville" (1977)
- "Cheeseburger in Paradise" (1978)
- "Son of a Son of a Sailor" (1979)
- "Fins" (1979)
- "Volcano" (1979)
- "Come Monday" (1974)
- "Why Don't We Get Drunk" (1973)
- "Changes in Latitudes, Changes in Attitudes" (1977)
- "Boat Drinks" (1979)
- "Pencil Thin Mustache" (1977)
- "A Pirate Looks at Forty" (1974)
- "One Particular Harbour" (1983)
- "Last Mango in Paris" (1986)
- "It's Five O'Clock Somewhere" (with Alan Jackson) (2003)
- "Knee Deep" (with Zac Brown Band) (2010)

Collaborations:

- "It's Five O'Clock Somewhere" (with Alan Jackson) (2003)
- "Knee Deep" (with Zac Brown Band) (2010)

This discography provides an overview of Jimmy Buffett's extensive musical career, including his albums, notable singles, and collaborations with other artists. It is a testament to his prolific output and enduring influence in the world of music.

B. Key Interviews and Quotes from Jimmy Buffett

Throughout his career, Jimmy Buffett has shared his insights, stories, and wisdom through interviews and public appearances. Here are some key interviews and memorable quotes from the man behind the Margaritaville lifestyle:

1. Interview with Rolling Stone (1974):

"I think about music as something that gets in and becomes a part of your life and becomes part of your chemistry. It's not a special thing that happens every time you get laid or you're on vacation or you're in the mood."

2. Interview with CBS Sunday Morning (2005):

"It's always been about escapism. It's always been about not taking yourself too seriously. You know, having a good time. I think you can have serious fun."

3. Interview with CMT (Country Music Television) Insider (2008):

"Music is always there. It's a constant. It's always been the most fun for me because it's allowed me to be more of a storyteller."

4. Interview with CBS This Morning (2013):

"The music's always been what drives me. I mean, I didn't wake up one day and go, 'I think I'll be a great businessman and open a chain of restaurants.' It happened because of the music."

5. Interview with Parade Magazine (2019):

"My job is to create a little pause in people's lives, to be able to have a little escapism and have some fun. That's my job."

6. Interview with The New York Times (2021):

"You've got to be passionate about what you're doing, or it's just a job. I've been fortunate to have a life that's not like that."

These interviews and quotes provide a glimpse into Jimmy Buffett's perspective on music, life, and the Margaritaville philosophy. They capture his enduring passion for storytelling, his commitment to having fun, and his belief in the power of music to bring joy and escapism to people's lives.

C. Glossary of Terms

Parrotheads: The dedicated and passionate fan community of Jimmy Buffett. Parrotheads are known for their love of Jimmy's music, their enthusiasm for the Margaritaville lifestyle, and their penchant for dressing in Hawaiian shirts, leis, and straw hats at his concerts.

Margaritaville: A fictional place and state of mind created by Jimmy Buffett in his music. It represents an idyllic tropical paradise where life is carefree, worries are left behind, and the pursuit of happiness takes center stage. Margaritaville has become a brand encompassing restaurants, resorts, merchandise, and a way of life.

Gulf and Western: A term often used to describe Jimmy Buffett's genre-defying musical style, which combines elements of folk, country, rock, and tropical rhythms. It reflects the influence of the Gulf Coast and the Caribbean on his music.

Trop Rock: Short for "tropical rock," it refers to a genre of music that incorporates elements of island and beach culture. Jimmy Buffett is often considered a pioneer of Trop Rock, known for his songs that transport listeners to beachfront destinations.

Steel Drum: A musical instrument commonly associated with Caribbean and tropical music. It produces melodic and rhythmic sounds and is often used in Jimmy Buffett's music to create a tropical atmosphere.

Parrothead Nation: A term used to describe the collective community of Parrotheads. It represents the shared love for Jimmy Buffett's music and the Margaritaville lifestyle among his fans.

Latitude Adjustment: A playful term used by Parrotheads to describe the feeling of relaxation and escape that comes with immersing oneself in Jimmy Buffett's music and the Margaritaville philosophy.

Fins Up: A hand gesture commonly associated with Parrotheads, where fans raise their hands with their fingers forming a fin-like shape, mimicking the shark fins mentioned in Jimmy Buffett's song "Fins."

LandShark: A brand of beer associated with Jimmy Buffett's Margaritaville brand. It reflects the coastal and tropical theme of his music and lifestyle.

Cheeseburger in Paradise: A popular Jimmy Buffett song that celebrates the simple pleasure of enjoying a cheeseburger in a tropical setting. It has become a symbol of the Margaritaville lifestyle.

Buffettology: A term coined to describe the study and appreciation of Jimmy Buffett's music, lyrics, and philosophy, often undertaken by dedicated Parrotheads.

This glossary provides definitions of key terms and phrases associated with Jimmy Buffett's music, lifestyle, and fan community, offering insights into the unique world he has created over the course of his career.

D. Selected Bibliography and Further Reading

Buffett, Jimmy. "A Pirate Looks at Fifty." Random House, 1998.

- Jimmy Buffett's autobiography offers a firsthand account of his life, adventures, and insights into his career and the Margaritaville lifestyle.

White, Tom Corcoran. "Jimmy Buffett: A Good Life All the Way." Touchstone, 2018.

- This biography provides an in-depth look at Jimmy Buffett's life and career, exploring his influences, music, and cultural impact.

Hiaasen, Carl. "Buffett: A Biography." Putnam Adult, 1997.

- Written by acclaimed author Carl Hiaasen, this biography delves into Jimmy Buffett's life, music, and the Gulf Coast culture that shaped him.

Cate, Spike. "The Parrothead Handbook: An Irreverent Guide to the Pirate in All of Us." Villard, 2002.

- Spike Cate's book offers an entertaining look at the Parrothead fan community, their traditions, and their love for Jimmy Buffett's music.

Rohter, Larry. "Margaritaville: The Romance and Reality of the Escapist's Paradise." St. Martin's Press, 2007.

- Larry Rohter explores the cultural phenomenon of Margaritaville and its impact on society, as inspired by Jimmy Buffett's music and lifestyle.

Bufwack, Mary A., and Robert K. Oermann. "Finding Her Voice: Women in Country Music, 1800-2000." Vanderbilt University Press, 2003.

- This book includes insights into Jimmy Buffett's collaborations with female country artists, providing a broader perspective on his contributions to music.

Smith, Michael Buffalo. "Rebel Yell: An Oral History of Southern Rock." Backbeat Books, 2014.

- Offers insights into Jimmy Buffett's role in the Southern rock music scene and his connections with other notable artists of the genre.

Various interviews and articles in music magazines and publications, including Rolling Stone, Billboard, and Entertainment Weekly, provide valuable historical context and interviews with Jimmy Buffett over the years.

These selected readings offer a comprehensive exploration of Jimmy Buffett's life, music, and the cultural impact of the Margaritaville lifestyle. They provide both fans and enthusiasts with a deeper understanding of the man behind the music and the philosophy he embodies.

Acknowledgments

Writing a comprehensive biography is a journey filled with research, dedication, and passion, and it would not be possible without the contributions and support of many individuals and resources.

First and foremost, I would like to express my gratitude to Jimmy Buffett for sharing his life's story, music, and Margaritaville philosophy with the world. His artistry and creativity have inspired countless individuals, and this biography is a tribute to his enduring legacy.

I would also like to extend my appreciation to the dedicated fans of Jimmy Buffett, the Parrotheads, who have celebrated his music and way of life with unwavering enthusiasm. Your love and support have helped shape this biography.

To the authors, journalists, and researchers who have chronicled Jimmy Buffett's journey and provided valuable insights, thank you for your dedication to preserving the history and culture surrounding this remarkable artist.

To the publishing houses, libraries, and digital archives that have made a wealth of information and resources available, your contributions to the world of literature and knowledge are invaluable.

Lastly, I extend my gratitude to the readers of this biography. Your interest in the life and career of Jimmy Buffett is a testament to the enduring power of music and storytelling.

This biography is a collective effort, and I am grateful to each and every individual and resource that has played a part in its creation. Thank you for joining me on this journey through the life and music of Jimmy Buffett.

Made in United States
Orlando, FL
08 April 2025